T0088425

JOHN RUTTER

THREE SHAKESPEARE SONGS

FOR MIXED VOICES UNACCOMPANIED

1.	O mistress mine	3
2.	Be not afeard	9
3.	Sigh no more, ladies	15

OXFORD

OXFORD
UNIVERSITY PRESS

Great Clarendon Street, Oxford OX2 6DP,
United Kingdom

Oxford University Press is a department of the University of Oxford.
It furthers the University's objective of excellence in research, scholarship,
and education by publishing worldwide. Oxford is a registered trade mark of
Oxford University Press in the UK and in certain other countries

© Collegium Music Publications 2022
Exclusively licensed worldwide to Oxford University Press

John Rutter has asserted his right under the Copyright, Designs
and Patents Act, 1988, to be identified as the Composer of this Work

First published 2022

Impression: 1

All rights reserved. No part of this publication may be reproduced,
stored in a retrieval system, or transmitted, in any form or by any means,
without the prior permission in writing of Oxford University Press

Permission to perform this work in public (except in the course of
divine worship) should normally be obtained from a local performing right
licensing organization, unless the owner or the occupier of the premises
being used already holds a licence from such an organization.
Likewise, permission to make and exploit a recording of this work
should be obtained from a local mechanical copyright licensing organization

Enquiries concerning reproduction outside the scope of the above
should be directed to the Music Rights Department, Oxford University Press, at
music.permissions.uk@oup.com or at the address above

ISBN 978–0–19–356247–9

Music originated on Sibelius
Printed in Great Britain on acid-free paper by
Halstan & Co. Ltd, Amersham, Bucks.

for Mark Ford and the Purcell Singers

THREE SHAKESPEARE SONGS

JOHN RUTTER

1. O mistress mine

Twelfth Night, Act II scene 3

* Dotted rhythms should be relaxed, like triplets.

© Collegium Music Publications 2022. Exclusively licensed worldwide to Oxford University Press.

Printed in Great Britain

OXFORD UNIVERSITY PRESS MUSIC DEPARTMENT, GREAT CLARENDON STREET, OXFORD OX2 6DP

The Moral Rights of the Composer have been asserted. Photocopying this copyright material is ILLEGAL.

*The melody line, in the tenor part, is omitted from here until bar 26 and between bars 42 and 44, in the interests of playability.

17
pp
Trip no fur - ther, pret - ty sweet - ing, Jour - neys end in
p
Trip no fur - ther, pret - ty sweet - ing, Jour - neys end
mp
più legato
Trip no fur - ther, pret - ty sweet - ing; Jour - neys end in
Trip no fur - ther, pret - ty sweet - ing, Jour - neys end in
Trip no fur - ther, pret - ty sweet - ing, Jour - neys end in
22
cresc.
mf
mp
love, Ev - 'ry wise man's son . . . Doo doo doo,
in love, Oo Doo doo doo,
lov - ers meet - ing, Ev - 'ry wise man's son doth know.
love, Oo Doo doo doo,
love, Oo Doo doo doo

27
mp
doo doo doo. 2. What is love? 'tis not here - af - ter; Pre - sent
p
doo doo doo. 2. What is love? not here - af - ter; Pre - sent
p
doo doo doo. 2. What is love? not here - af - ter; Pre - sent
p
doo doo doo. 2. What is love? not here - af - ter; Pre - sent
p
doo doo doo doo doo doo doo doo doo doo doo doo
mp
31
cresc.
mf
mirth hath pre - sent laugh - ter; What's to come is still un -
mirth hath pre - sent laugh - ter; What's to come is still un -
mirth hath pre - sent laugh - ter; What's to come is still un -
mirth hath pre - sent laugh - ter; What's to come is still un -
doo doo doo doo, What's to come is still un -

36
poco a poco rall.
rit.
p
-sure, still un - sure:
- sure, still, still un - sure:
mp
- sure, still un - sure, still un - sure:
- sure, still un - sure, still un - sure: Ah,
-sure, still un - sure, still un - sure:
poco a poco rall.
rit.
42
a tempo
mp
In de - lay lies no plen - ty; Then come kiss me,
mf warmly
In de - lay lies no plen - ty; Then come kiss me,
mf cantabile
In de - lay there lies no plen - ty; Then come kiss me,
warmly
In de - lay lies no plen - ty; Then come kiss me,
Doo doo doo doo doo doo doo Then come kiss me,
a tempo

47
mp
sweet and twen - ty, Youth's a stuff will not en - dure,
sweet and twen - ty, Youth's a stuff will not en - dure, not en - dure,
sweet and twen - ty, Oo not en - dure,
sweet and twen - ty, Oo not en - dure,
sweet and twen - ty, Oo doo doo doo doo
52
rall.
dim.
Un poco lento
p
youth's a stuff will not en - dure, en - dure.
Più lento
pp
not en - dure, Hum en - dure.
not en - dure, Hum en - dure.
not en - dure, Hum en - dure.
doo doo doo, en - dure, en - dure.

2. Be not afeard

The Tempest, Act III scene 2

*These three voice parts should be balanced equally. The 2nd soprano part may be taken by 1st altos, or other reassignments of individual voices applied.

7
p
pp
full of noi - ses, Sounds and sweet airs, that give de -
(open slightly)
13
mp
mf
- light, and hurt not. Some - times a thou - sand
ah
cresc.

19
mp
twan - gling in - stru - ments Will hum a - bout mine
twan - gling in - stru - ments Will hum a - bout mine
twan - gling in - stru - ments Will hum a - bout mine
twan - gling in - - - - stru - ments hum (m) a - bout mine
twan - gling in - - - - stru - ments hum (m) a - bout mine
24
p
ears; and some - time voi - ces,
ears; and some - time voi - ces,
ears; and some - time voi - ces, That, if I then had
cresc.
and voi - ces, voi - -
(p)
ears; and some - time voi - ces, That, if I then had
ears; voi - ces, voi - -

28
mp
p
af - ter long sleep, Will make me sleep a - gain,
af - ter long sleep, Will make me sleep a - gain,
waked af - ter long sleep, Will make me sleep a - gain,
(p)
- ces, voi - - ces, sleep, sleep, sleep,
waked af - ter long sleep, sleep, sleep
- ces, voi - - ces, sleep, sleep,
33
pp
sleep a - gain: and then, in dream - ing, The
sleep a - gain: and then, in dream - ing, The
sleep a - gain: and then, in dream - ing, The
sleep, sleep a - gain: in dream, dream - - ing,
a - gain, sleep a - gain: and then, in dream, dream - ing,
sleep a - gain: in dream, dream - ing,

38
poco stringendo
Poco più mosso
♩ = 92
poco a poco cresc.
mf
clouds me - thought would o - pen and show rich - es
Ah
ah
show
43
poco rallentando
Tempo I
mp
pp
Rea - dy to drop up - on me;
that, when I
Hum
- es

48
p
mp
waked, when I waked I cried to dream a - gain,
waked, when I waked I cried to dream a - gain,
waked, when I waked I cried to dream a - gain,
when I waked, that when I waked Hum
when I waked, that when I waked Hum
when I waked, that when I waked Hum
53
rit. al fine
pp
dim. a niente
to dream a - gain, to dream a - gain.
to dream a - gain, to dream a - gain.
to dream a - gain, to dream a - gain.

3. Sigh no more, ladies

Much Ado about Nothing, Act II scene 3

7
mf
1. Sigh no more, la - dies, sigh no more, Men were de -
mf
sigh no more, Sigh no more, la - dies, sigh no more, Men were de -
dim.
mp
more, oh, oh, oh,
dim.
mp
no more, oh, oh, oh, oh, oh,
dim.
mp
dm dm dm dm dm dm dm dm
dim.
mp
mf
14
-ceiv - ers ev - er; One foot in sea, and one on shore, To
-ceiv - ers ev - er; One foot in sea, and one on shore, To
oh, oh, oh,
oh, oh, ev - er, oh, oh, oh,
dm dm dm dm dm dm dm dm

21
mp
one thing con - stant nev - er. Then sigh not so, But let them
p
one thing con - stant nev - er. Oh, oh, oh,
p
one thing con - stant nev - er. Oh, oh, oh,
p
one thing con - stant, no nev - er. Oh, oh, oh,
p
dm dm dm oh, oh,
mp
28
cresc. poco a poco
go, And be you blithe and bon - ny, Con - vert - ing all your
cresc. poco a poco
be you blithe and bon - ny, Con - vert - ing all your
cresc. poco a poco
oh, oh, oh, oh, Con - vert - ing all your
cresc. poco a poco
oh, oh, oh, oh, Con - vert - ing all your
cresc. poco a poco
oh, oh, oh, Con - vert - ing all your
cresc. poco a poco

35
f ma leggiero
sounds of woe In - to Hey non - ny, non - ny, hey non - ny, non - ny, hey non - ny,
mf leggiero
sounds of woe In - to Hey non - ny, hey non - ny, hey
mf leggiero
sounds of woe, Hey non - ny, hey non - ny, hey
mf leggiero
sounds of woe, Hey non - ny, hey non - ny, hey
mf leggiero
sounds of woe, Hey non - ny, hey non - ny, hey
f ma leggiero
42
non - ny,
mf
non - ny, non - ny no, Hey non - ny, non - ny, hey non - ny, non - ny,
non - ny, non - ny, non - ny, Hey non - ny, non - ny, hey non - ny non - ny,
non - ny, non - ny, non - ny, Hey non - ny, non - ny, hey non - ny non - ny,
non - ny, non - ny, non - ny, Hey non - ny, non - ny, hey non - ny non - ny,
non - ny, non - ny, non - ny, hey non - ny, hey non - ny,
mf

*The melody line, in the tenor part, is omitted from here until bar 70 in the interests of playability.

63
mp
oh, oh, oh, oh oh.
mp
oh, oh, oh, oh, oh, oh, oh,
fraud of men was ev - er so, Since sum - mer first was leav - y,
Oh, oh, oh, oh, hey non - ny non - ny,
non - ny, non - ny, hey non - ny no.
70
mp
poco cresc.
mf
Then sigh not so, But let them go, And be you blithe and
p
poco cresc.
mp
oh, oh, And be you blithe and
p
poco cresc.
mp
oh, oh, be you
p
poco cresc.
mp
non - ny, oh, oh, be you
p
poco cresc.
mp
Oh, oh, be you
mp
poco cresc.
mf

77
p cresc.
mf
bon - ny, oh, oh, oh,
p cresc.
mf
(mf)
bon - ny, oh, oh, oh, oh, Hey,
p cresc.
mf
f
bon - ny, Con - vert - ing all your sounds of woe In - to Hey non - ny,
p cresc.
mf
bon - ny, oh, Con - vert - ing all your sounds of woe In - to Hey
p cresc.
mf
bon - ny, Con - vert - ing all your sounds of woe In - to Hey
p
cresc.
mf
f
84
hey, hey non - ny, non - ny,
non - ny, hey non - ny, non - ny, hey non - ny, non - ny, non - ny,
non - ny, hey non - ny, hey non - ny, non - ny, non - ny,
non - ny, hey non - ny, hey non - ny, non - ny,

23 April 2021
Shakespeare's birthday